THANK YOU!

FOR CHOOSING

CURSIVE HANDWRITING WORKBOOK

FOR KIDS & BEGINNERS

We value your opinion and would appreciate your feedback.

Your insights can help us improve future publications and

enhance the customer experience. Thank you for taking the

time to share your thoughts with us.

Chika C. & Creo Images

CURSIVE HANDWRITING WORKBOOK

FOR KIDS & BEGINNERS

CHIKA C. & CREO IMAGES

Who is This Book For?

This workbook is for beginners and kids 6 and up, providing a fun, flexible and progressive approach to learning cursive writing.

- Students can use the standard pencil, light color marker or a pen for the writing

- To add color, crayons and colored pencils are amazing for the coloring activities

With the help of this workbook you will learn to write in cursive in 3 easy steps:

1. Learn to trace and write the uppercase and lowercase letters

2. Trace and practice letters in word formation

3. Trace and practice writing full sentences

Have fun coloring any pictures in the book!

You got this and Happy Learning!

Chika C. & Creo Images

This Book Belongs to

This Cursive Handwriting workbook is divided in the following parts:

Section 1

Learning the Cursive Alphabet

Trace and practice letters a-z and A-Z

Section 2

Writing words

Connecting simple words

Section 3

Writing simple sentences

Connecting words to form an entire sentence

Bonus Round

Longer Sentence practice and Jokes

Students can use a pencil, pen or a light color marker to trace the dotted letters and words

SECTION

1

Learning and Writing the Alphabet in Cursive.

Trace the letters and practice writing them in the remaining spaces!

Use the blank practice page to write on your own at the end

HOW TO WRITE LOWERCASE A

Trace inside the cursive letter by following the arrows

a a a a a a a a a

HOW TO WRITE UPPERCASE A

Trace inside the cursive letter by following the arrows

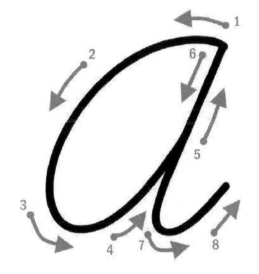

a a a a a a a a a

a a a a a a a

a a a a a a a

a a a

a

a a a a a a

a a a

a

PRACTICE SHEET

ANT

"No Matter how hard it is, I Can Do it"

HOW TO WRITE LOWERCASE B

Trace inside the cursive letter by following the arrows

𝑏 𝑏 𝑏 𝑏 𝑏 𝑏 𝑏 𝑏 𝑏 𝑏 𝑏

HOW TO WRITE UPPERCASE B

Trace inside the cursive letter by following the arrows

ℬ ℬ ℬ ℬ ℬ ℬ ℬ ℬ

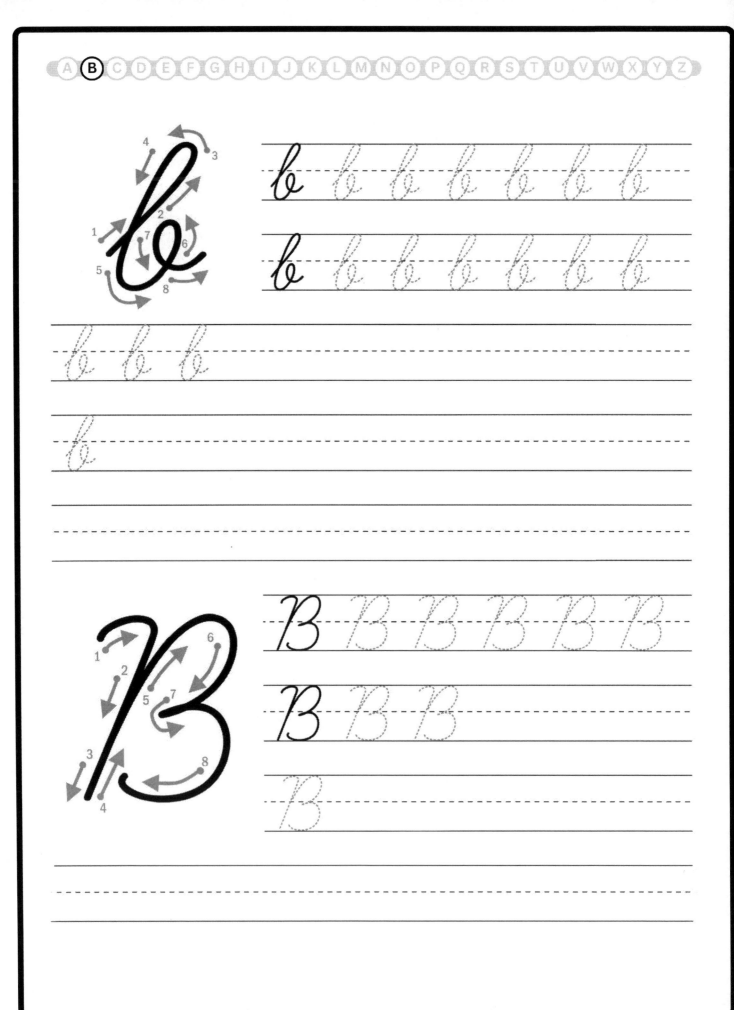

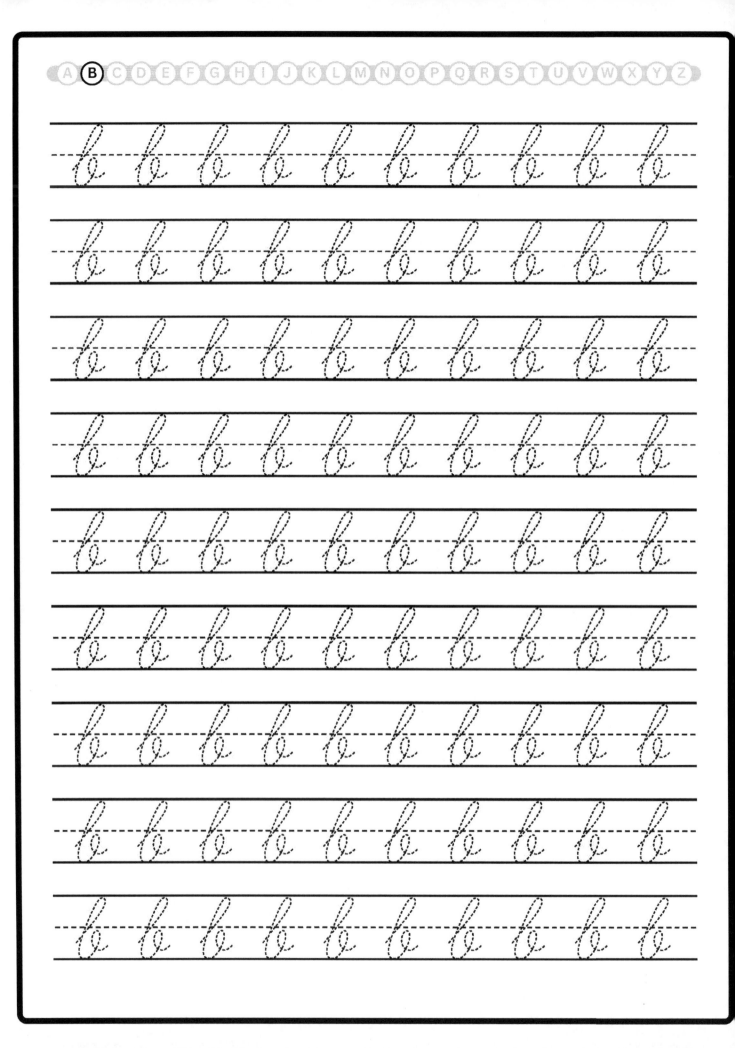

PRACTICE SHEET

BIRD

"Anything is Possible"

HOW TO WRITE LOWERCASE C

Trace inside the cursive letter by following the arrows

c c c c c c c c c c c c c

HOW TO WRITE UPPERCASE C

Trace inside the cursive letter by following the arrows

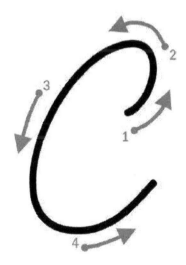

C C C C C C C C C C

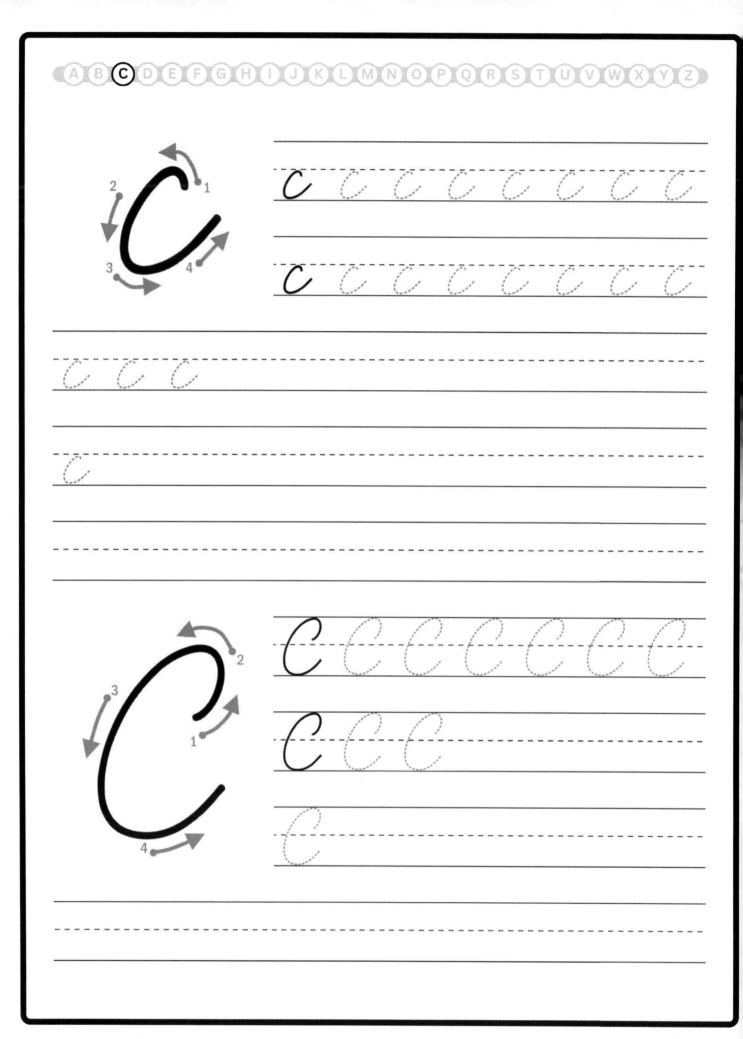

PRACTICE SHEET

CAT

"I go after my dreams"

HOW TO WRITE LOWERCASE D

Trace inside the cursive letter by following the arrows

d d d d d d d d d

HOW TO WRITE UPPERCASE D

Trace inside the cursive letter by following the arrows

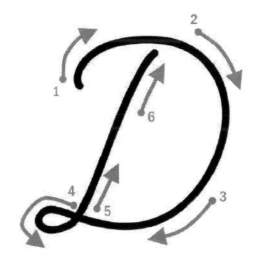

D D D D D D D

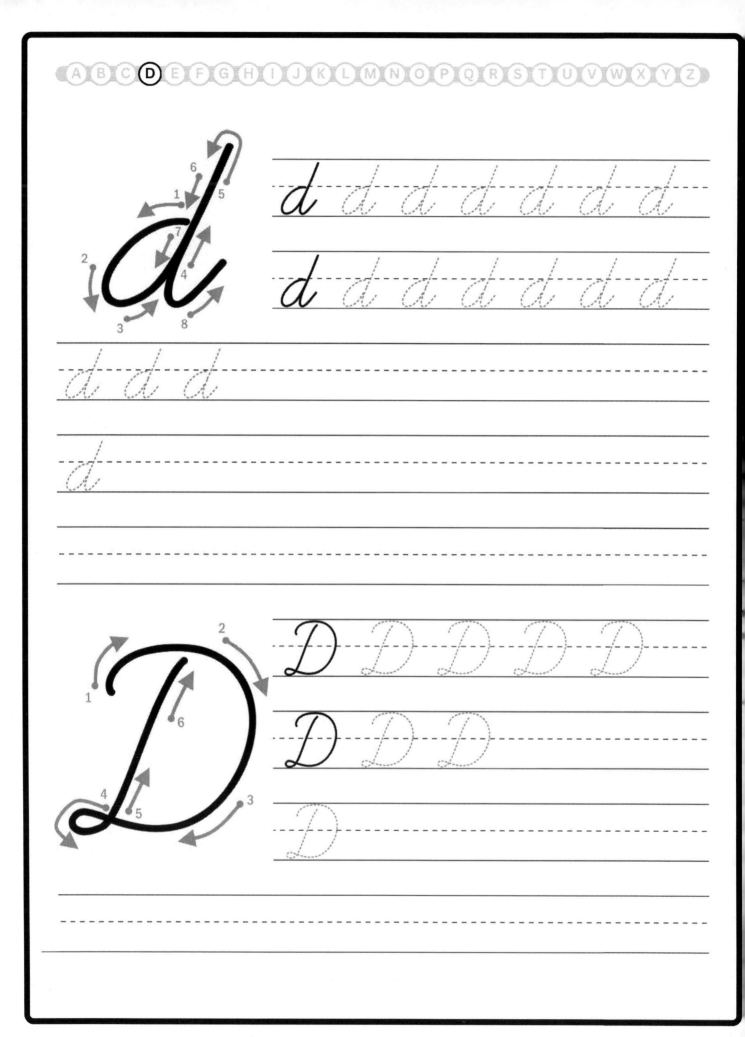

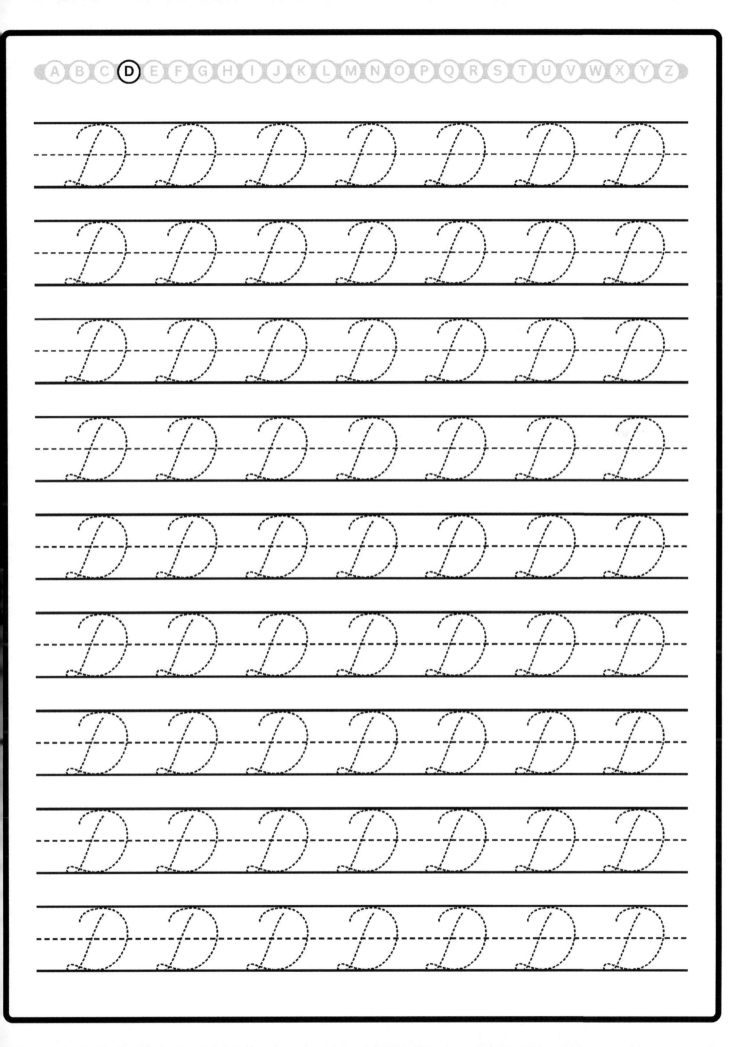

PRACTICE SHEET

DOG

"Mistakes help me learn and grow"

HOW TO WRITE LOWERCASE E

Trace inside the cursive letter by following the arrows

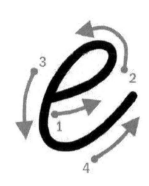

HOW TO WRITE UPPERCASE E

Trace inside the cursive letter by following the arrows

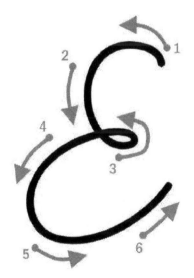

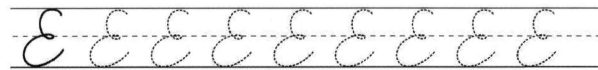

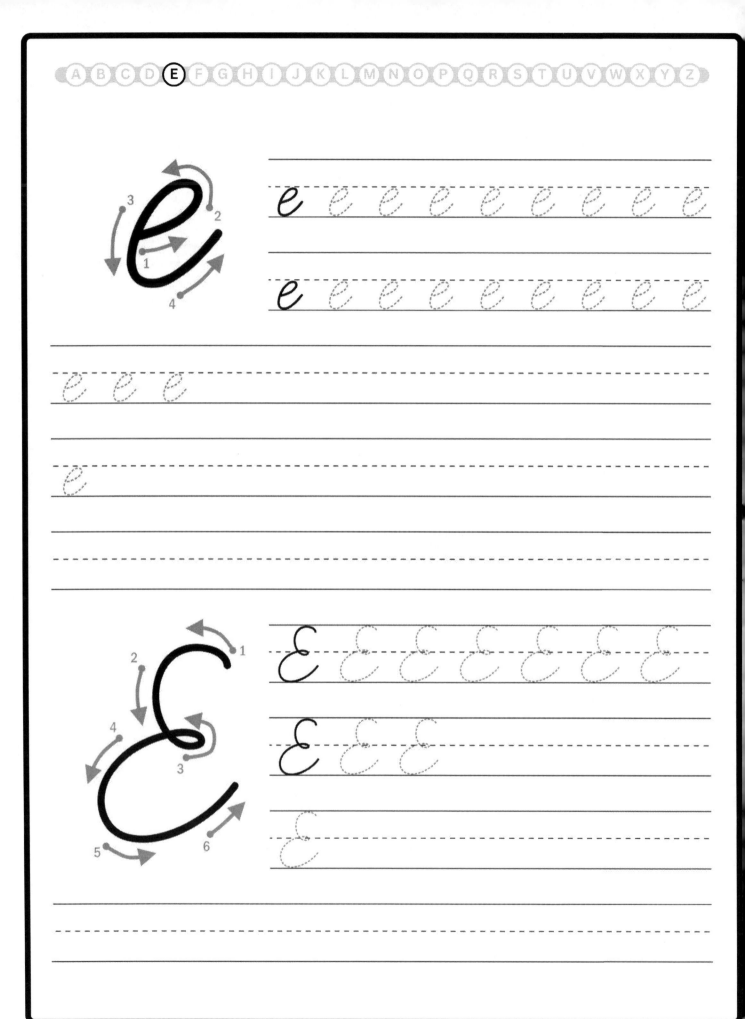

PRACTICE SHEET

ELEPHANT

"I am important and special"

HOW TO WRITE LOWERCASE F

Trace inside the cursive letter by following the arrows

f f f f f f f f f f

HOW TO WRITE UPPERCASE F

Trace inside the cursive letter by following the arrows

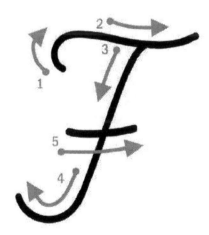

F F F F F F F F

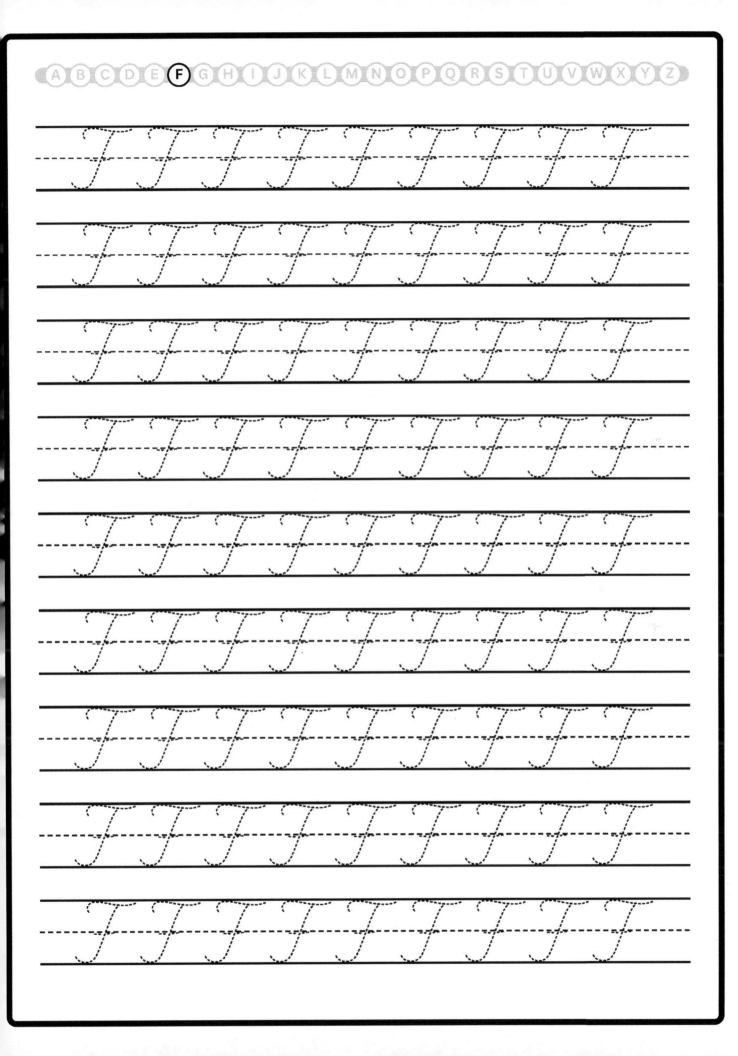

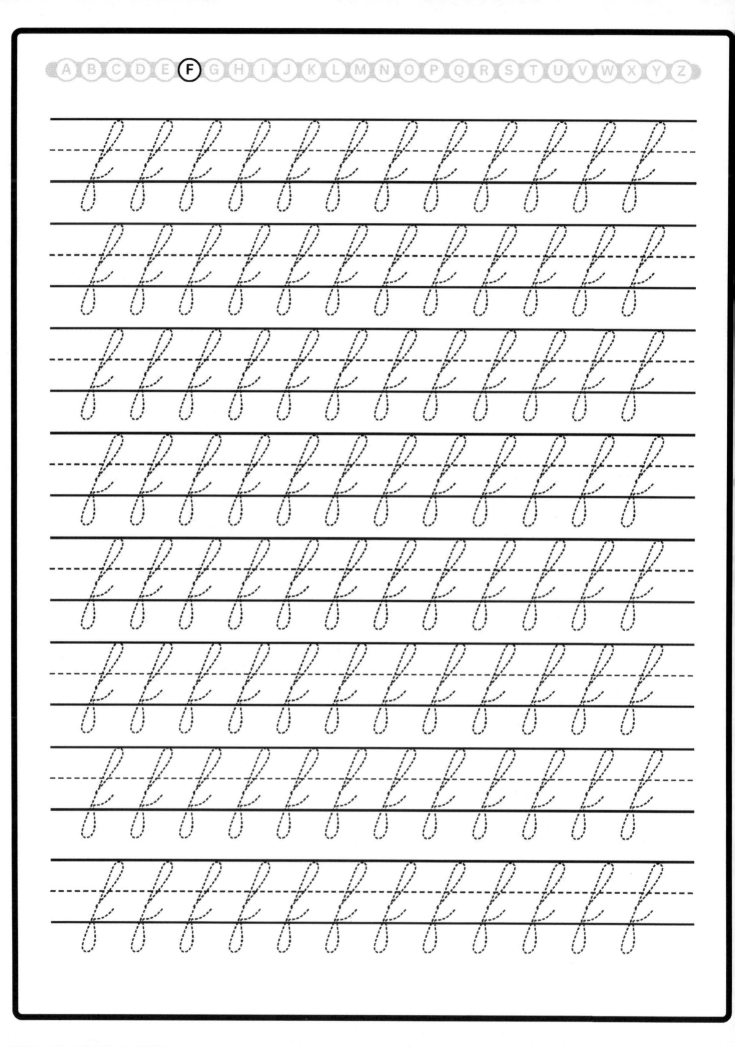

PRACTICE SHEET

FROG

"I am better every single day"

HOW TO WRITE LOWERCASE G

Trace inside the cursive letter by following the arrows

g g g g g g g g g g g

HOW TO WRITE UPPERCASE G

Trace inside the cursive letter by following the arrows

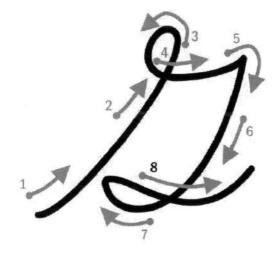

G G G G G G G

PRACTICE SHEET

GIRAFFE

"Everything will be okay"

HOW TO WRITE LOWERCASE H

Trace inside the cursive letter by following the arrows

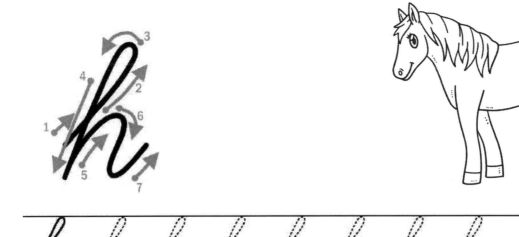

h h h h h h h h h

HOW TO WRITE UPPERCASE H

Trace inside the cursive letter by following the arrows

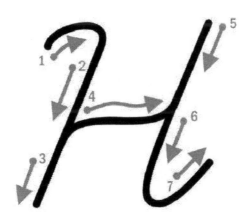

H H H H H H H

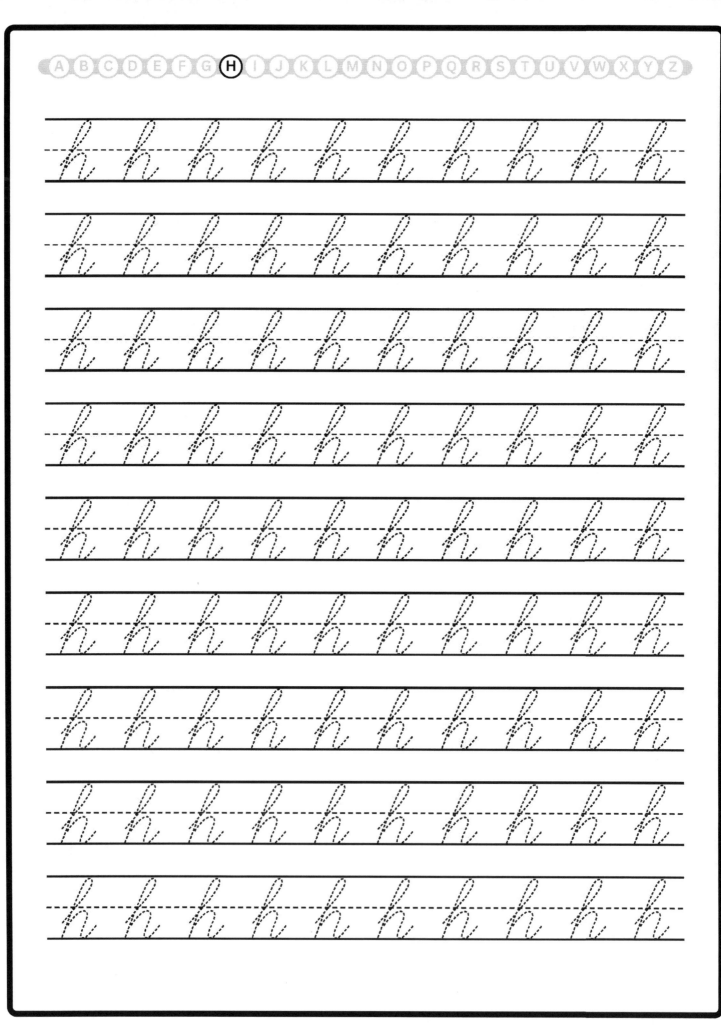

PRACTICE SHEET

HIPPO

"I can do better next time"

HOW TO WRITE LOWERCASE I

Trace inside the cursive letter by following the arrows

i i i i i i i i i i i i i i i i i

HOW TO WRITE UPPERCASE I

Trace inside the cursive letter by following the arrows

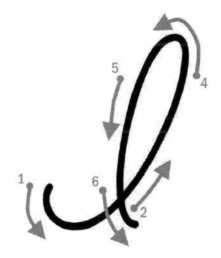

l l l l l l l l l l l l

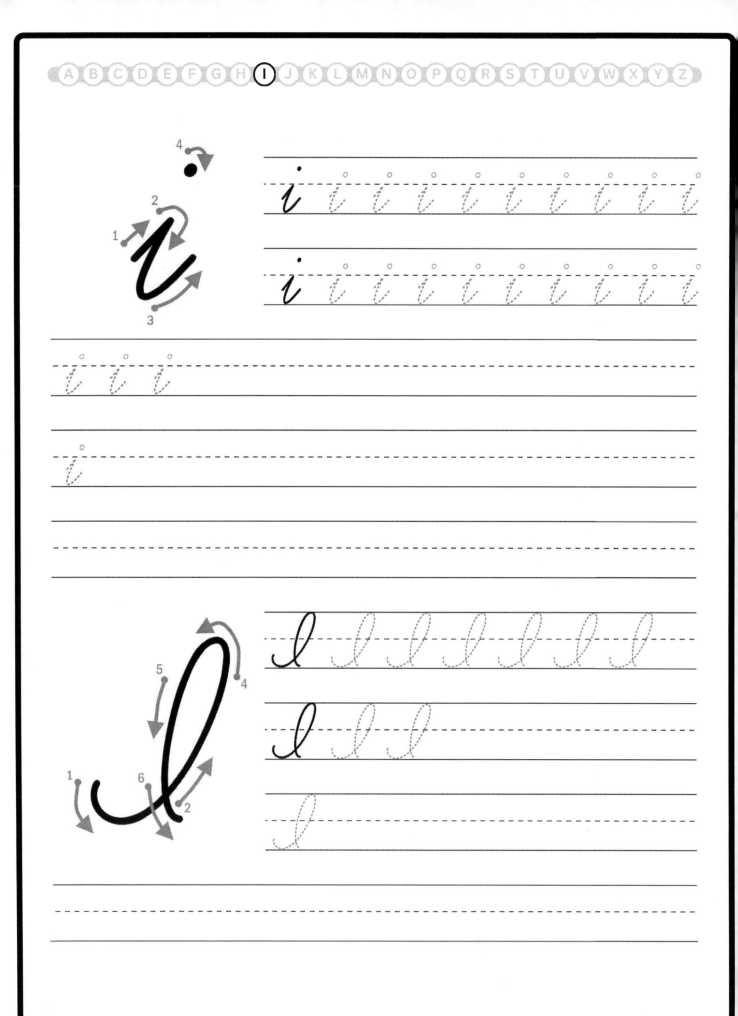

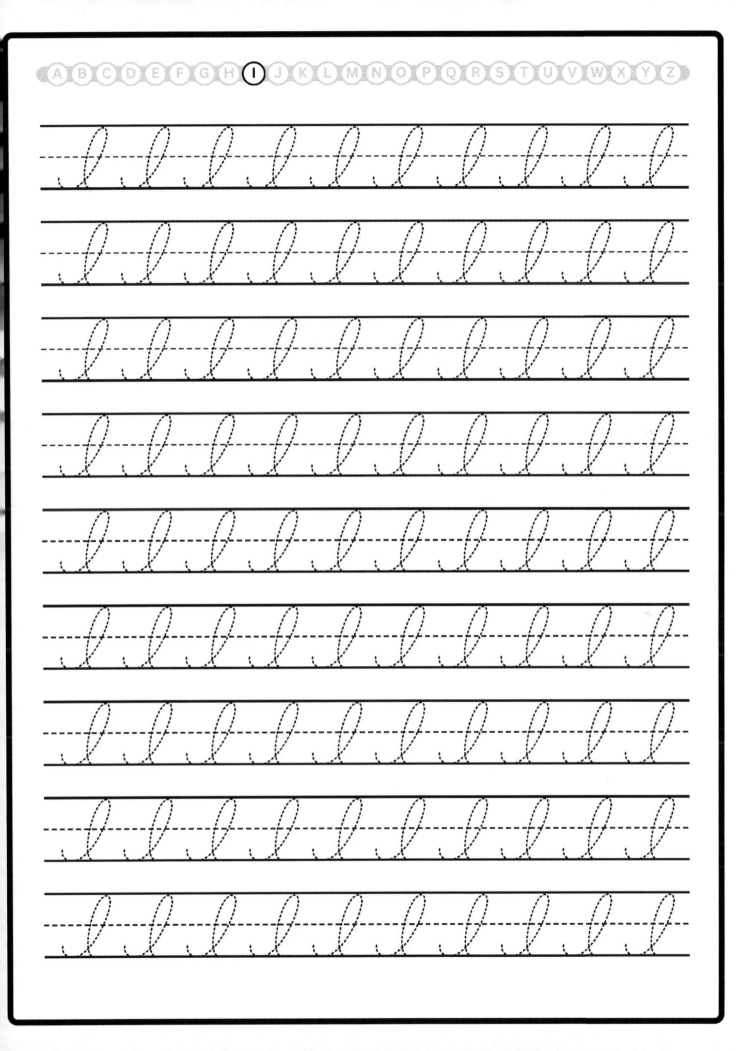

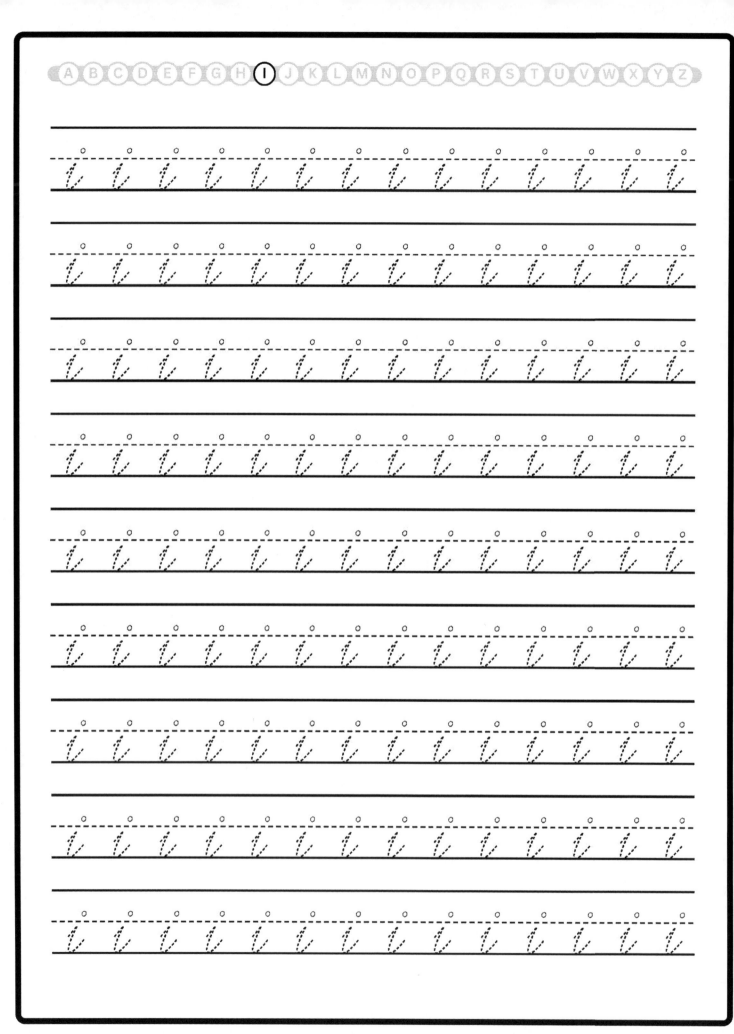

PRACTICE SHEET

IMPALA

"Today is going to be a great day"

HOW TO WRITE LOWERCASE J

Trace inside the cursive letter by following the arrows

j j j j j j j j j j j j j

HOW TO WRITE UPPERCASE J

Trace inside the cursive letter by following the arrows

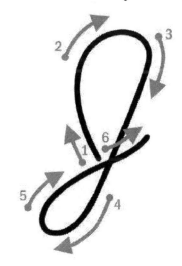

J J J J J J J J J

PRACTICE SHEET

JAGUAR

"I can make a difference"

HOW TO WRITE LOWERCASE K

Trace inside the cursive letter by following the arrows

k k k k k k k k k k k

HOW TO WRITE UPPERCASE K

Trace inside the cursive letter by following the arrows

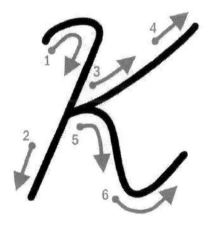

K K K K K K K K

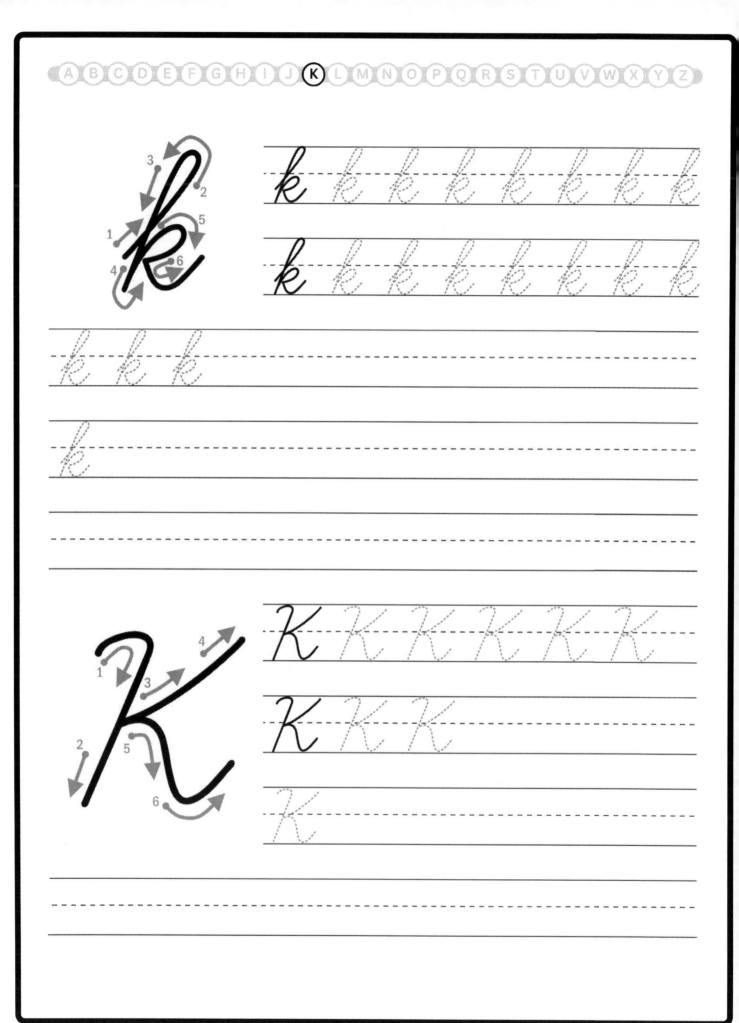

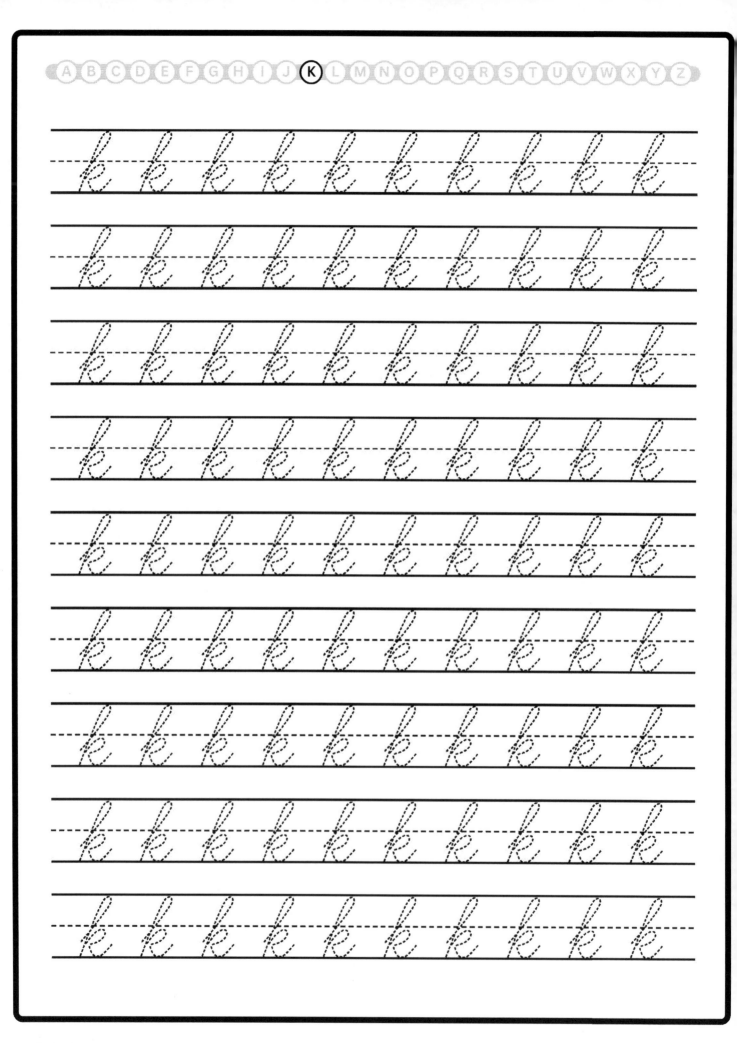

PRACTICE SHEET

KANGAROO

"I believe in myself and my abilities"

HOW TO WRITE LOWERCASE L

Trace inside the cursive letter by following the arrows

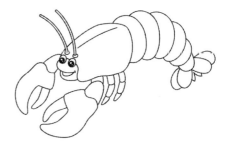

ℓ ℓ ℓ ℓ ℓ ℓ ℓ ℓ ℓ ℓ ℓ ℓ

HOW TO WRITE UPPERCASE L

Trace inside the cursive letter by following the arrows

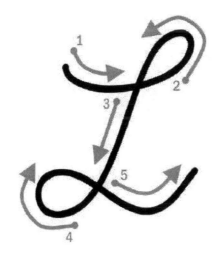

L L L L L L L L

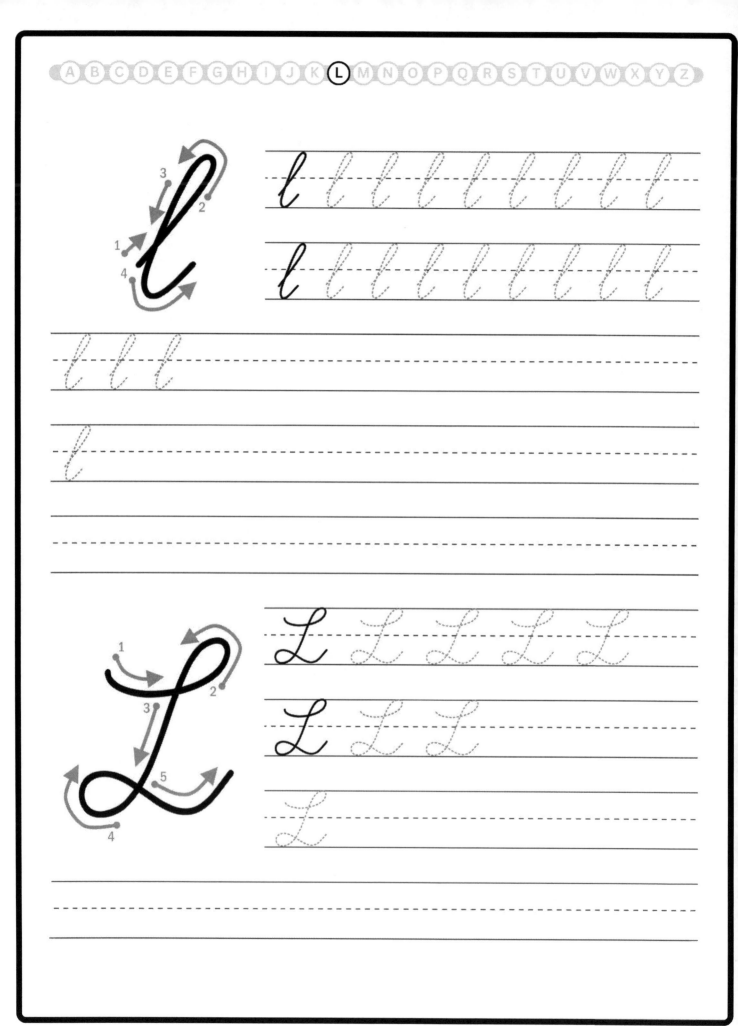

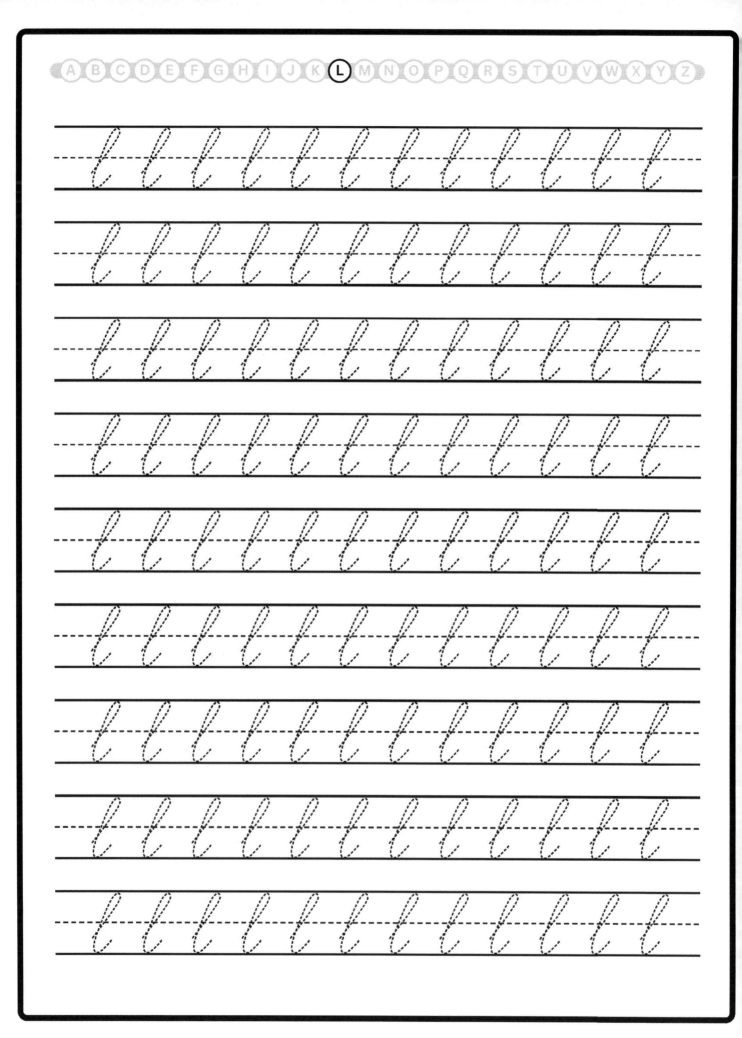

PRACTICE SHEET

LION

"Everyday is a fresh start"

HOW TO WRITE LOWERCASE M

Trace inside the cursive letter by following the arrows

m m m m m m

HOW TO WRITE UPPERCASE M

Trace inside the cursive letter by following the arrows

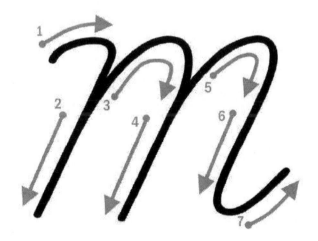

m m m m m m

m m m m m

m m m m m

m m m

m

M M M M M

M M M

M

PRACTICE SHEET

MONKEY

"I am strong and determined"

HOW TO WRITE LOWERCASE N

Trace inside the cursive letter by following the arrows

n n n n n n n n

HOW TO WRITE UPPERCASE N

Trace inside the cursive letter by following the arrows

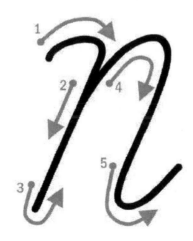

n n n n n n n n

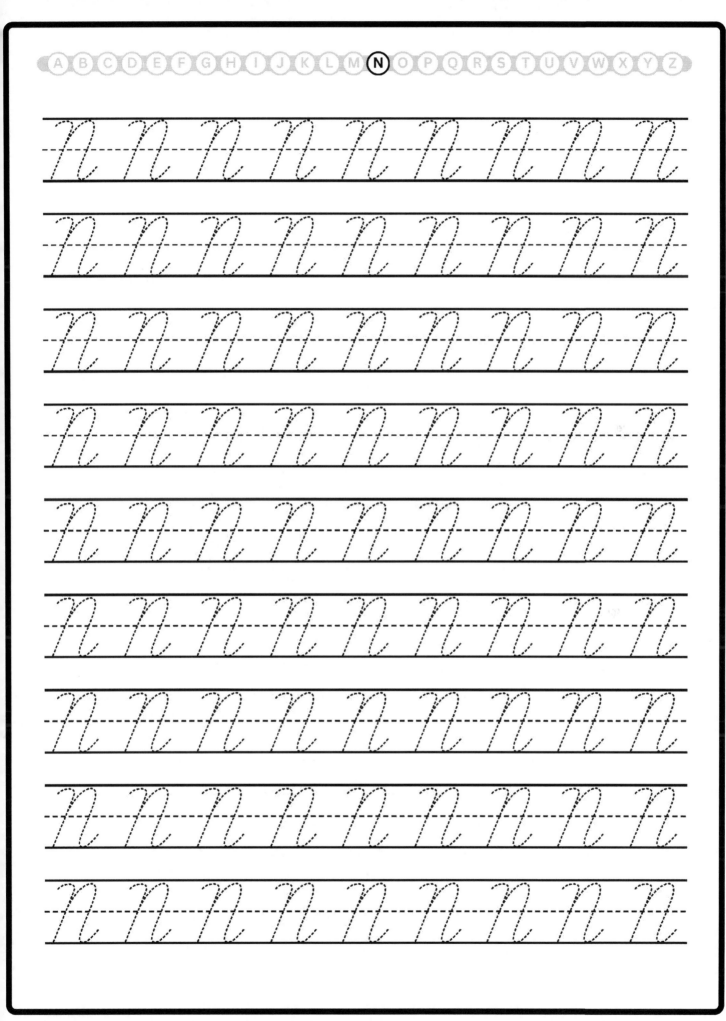

PRACTICE SHEET

NEWT

"I start with a positive mindset"

HOW TO WRITE LOWERCASE O

Trace inside the cursive letter by following the arrows

O O O O O O O O O O O

HOW TO WRITE UPPERCASE O

Trace inside the cursive letter by following the arrows

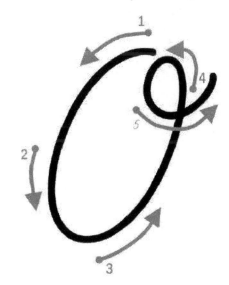

O O O O O O O O O O

O O O O O O O

O O O O O O O

O O O

O

O O O O O O O

O O O

O

PRACTICE SHEET

OWL

"Anything is Possible"

HOW TO WRITE LOWERCASE P

Trace inside the cursive letter by following the arrows

p p p p p p p p p p p

HOW TO WRITE UPPERCASE P

Trace inside the cursive letter by following the arrows

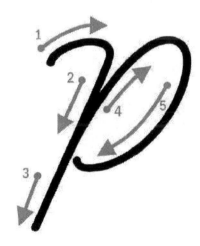

P P P P P P P P P P P

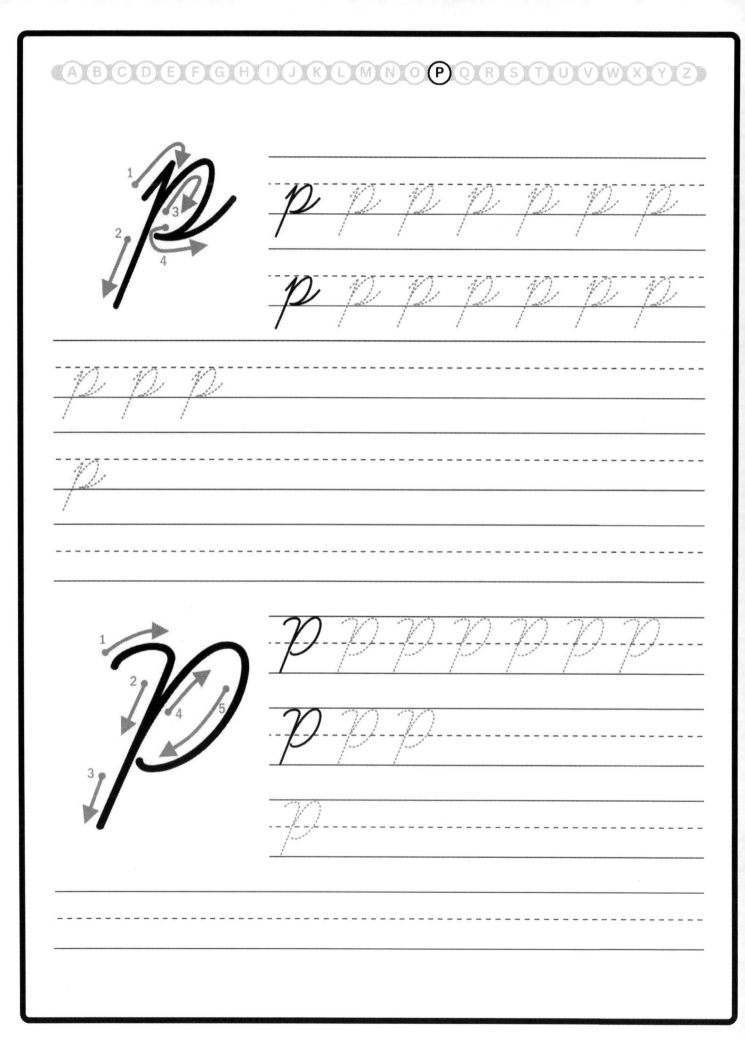

A B C D E F G H I J K L M N O P Q R S T U V W X Y Z

PRACTICE SHEET

PUMA

"I am thankful for today"

HOW TO WRITE LOWERCASE Q

Trace inside the cursive letter by following the arrows

q q q q q q q q q q q

HOW TO WRITE UPPERCASE Q

Trace inside the cursive letter by following the arrows

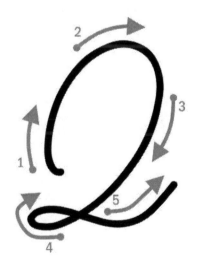

Q Q Q Q Q Q Q Q Q Q Q

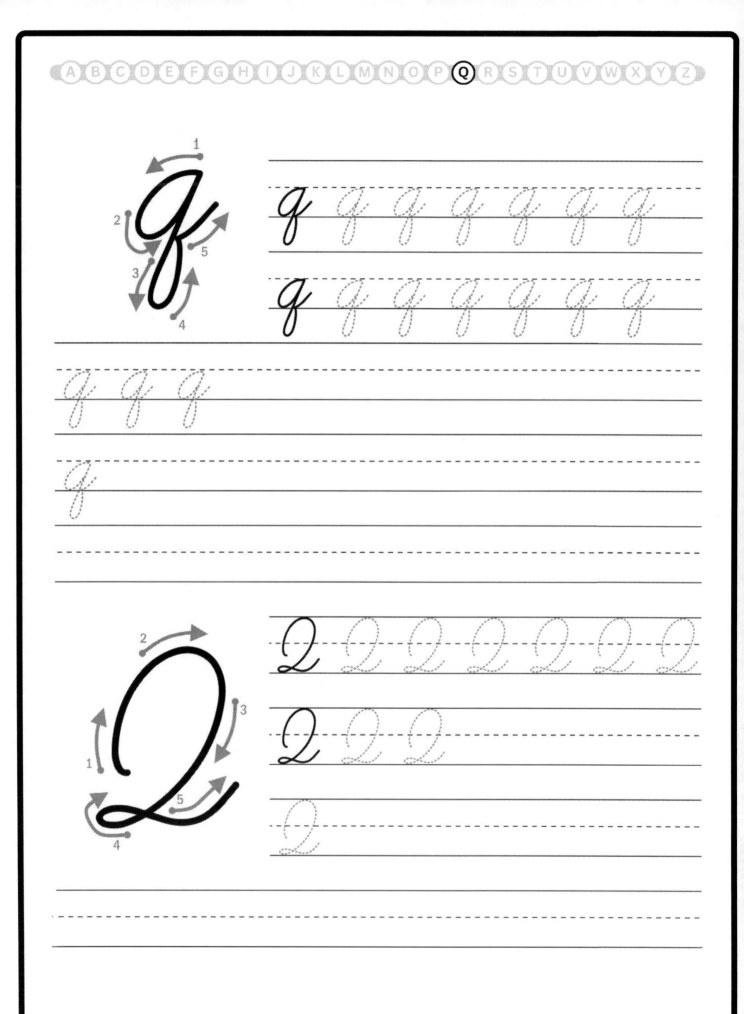

PRACTICE SHEET

QUOKKA

"I am working on my own pace"

HOW TO WRITE LOWERCASE R

Trace inside the cursive letter by following the arrows

HOW TO WRITE UPPERCASE R

Trace inside the cursive letter by following the arrows

PRACTICE SHEET

RHINOCEROS

"I am building my future"

HOW TO WRITE LOWERCASE S

Trace inside the cursive letter by following the arrows

HOW TO WRITE UPPERCASE S

Trace inside the cursive letter by following the arrows

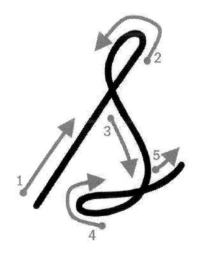

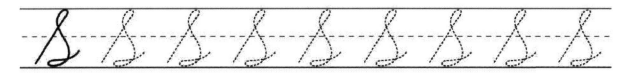

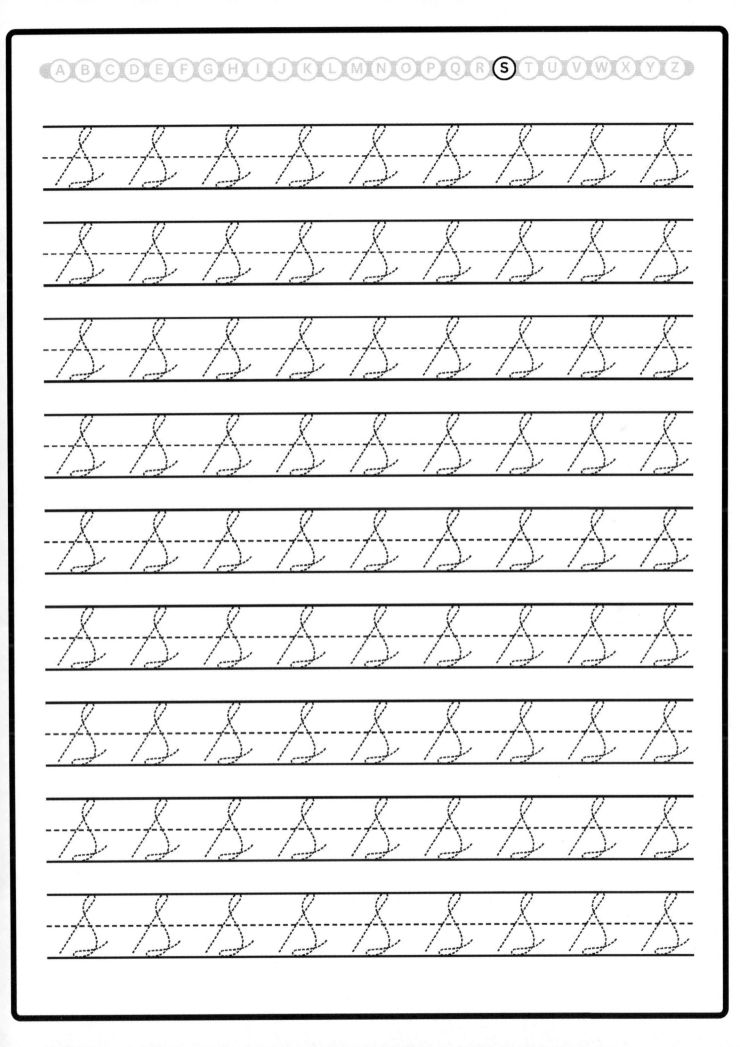

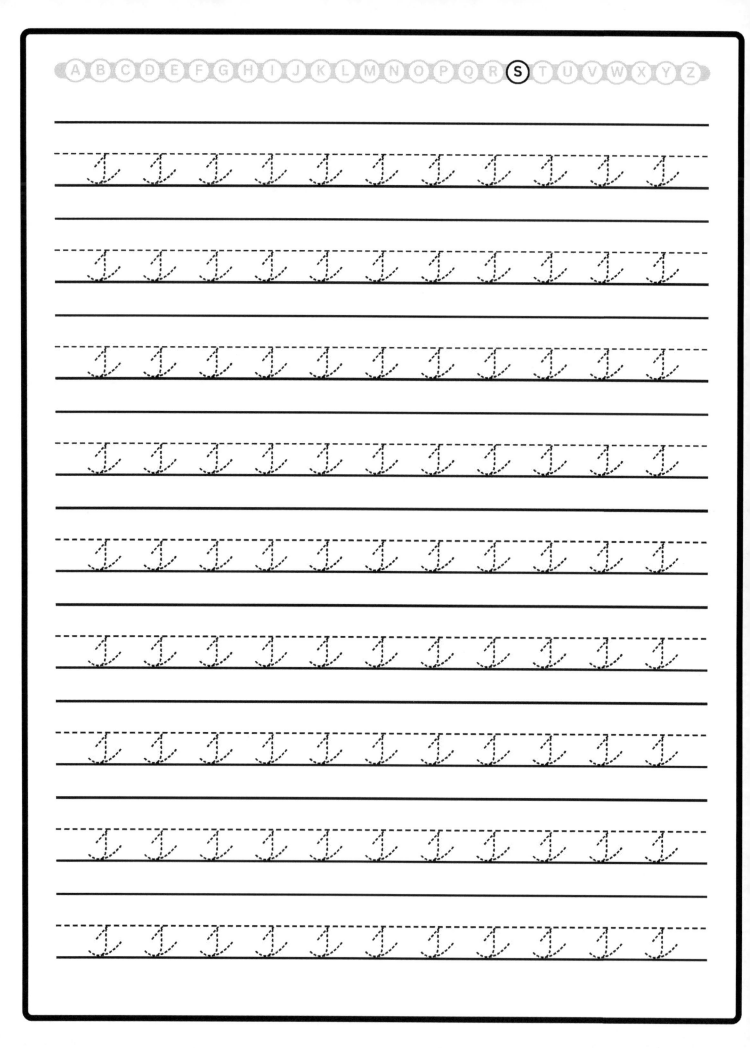

PRACTICE SHEET

SHEEP

"I am open and ready to learn"

HOW TO WRITE LOWERCASE T

Trace inside the cursive letter by following the arrows

t t t t t t t t t t t

HOW TO WRITE UPPERCASE T

Trace inside the cursive letter by following the arrows

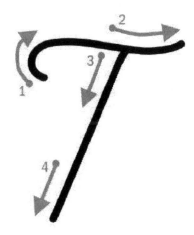

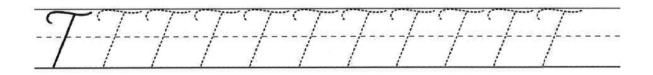

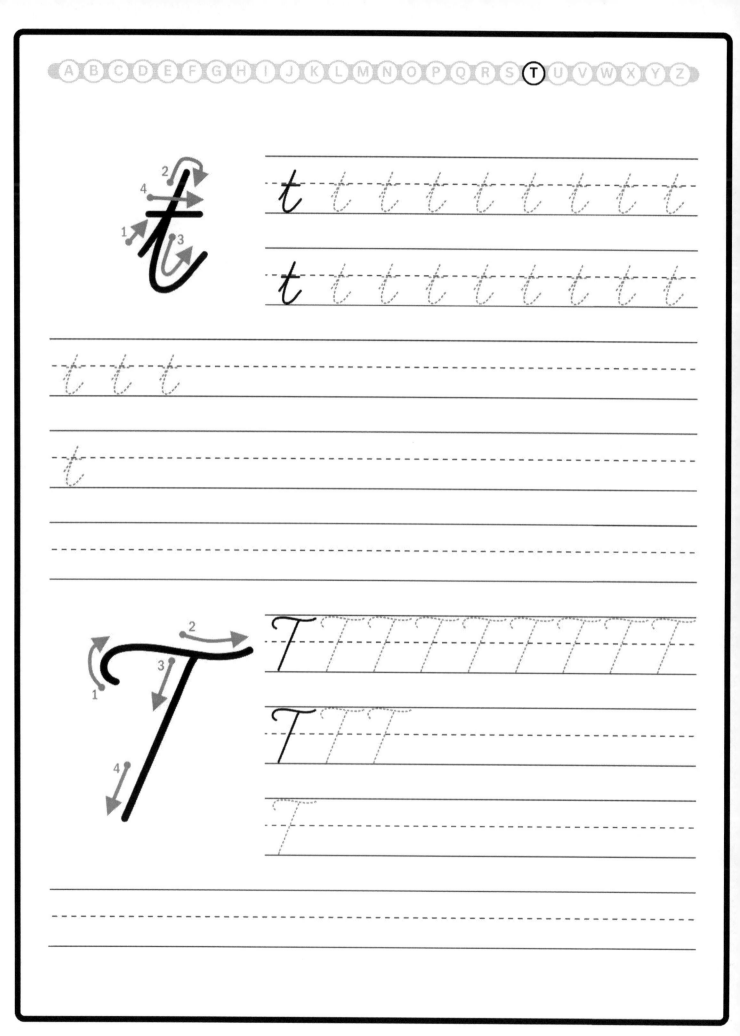

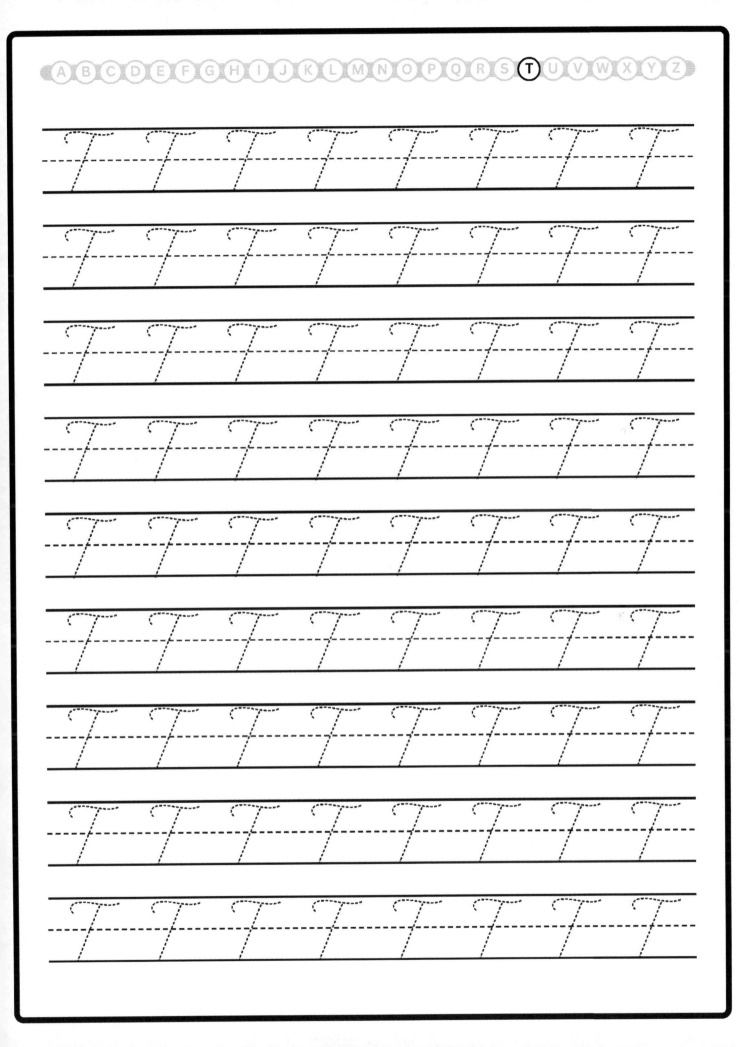

PRACTICE SHEET

TIGER

"I am open and ready to learn"

HOW TO WRITE LOWERCASE U

Trace inside the cursive letter by following the arrows

u u u u u u u u u u

HOW TO WRITE UPPERCASE U

Trace inside the cursive letter by following the arrows

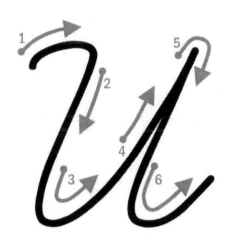

U U U U U U U

u u u u u u u u u

u u u u u u u u

u u u

u

U U U U U U

U U U

U

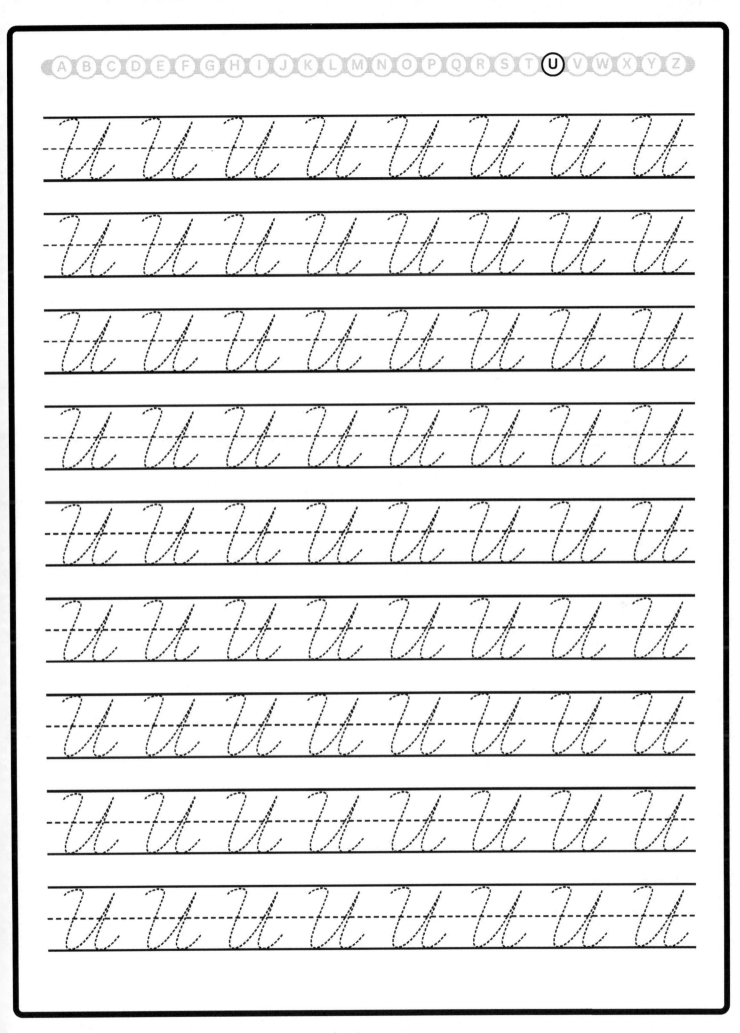

PRACTICE SHEET

UNICORN

"Today I am leader"

HOW TO WRITE LOWERCASE V

Trace inside the cursive letter by following the arrows

𝓊 𝓊 𝓊 𝓊 𝓊 𝓊 𝓊 𝓊

HOW TO WRITE UPPERCASE V

Trace inside the cursive letter by following the arrows

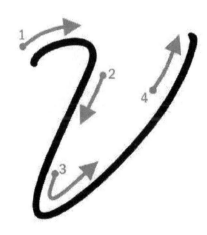

𝒱 𝒱 𝒱 𝒱 𝒱 𝒱 𝒱 𝒱 𝒱

A B C D E F G H I J K L M N O P Q R S T U V W X Y Z

PRACTICE SHEET

VERVET MONKEY

"I am a lifelong learner"

HOW TO WRITE LOWERCASE W

Trace inside the cursive letter by following the arrows

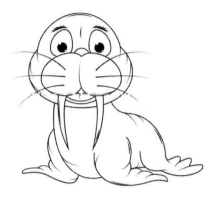

HOW TO WRITE UPPERCASE W

Trace inside the cursive letter by following the arrows

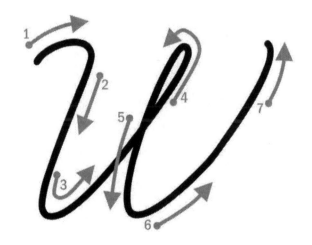

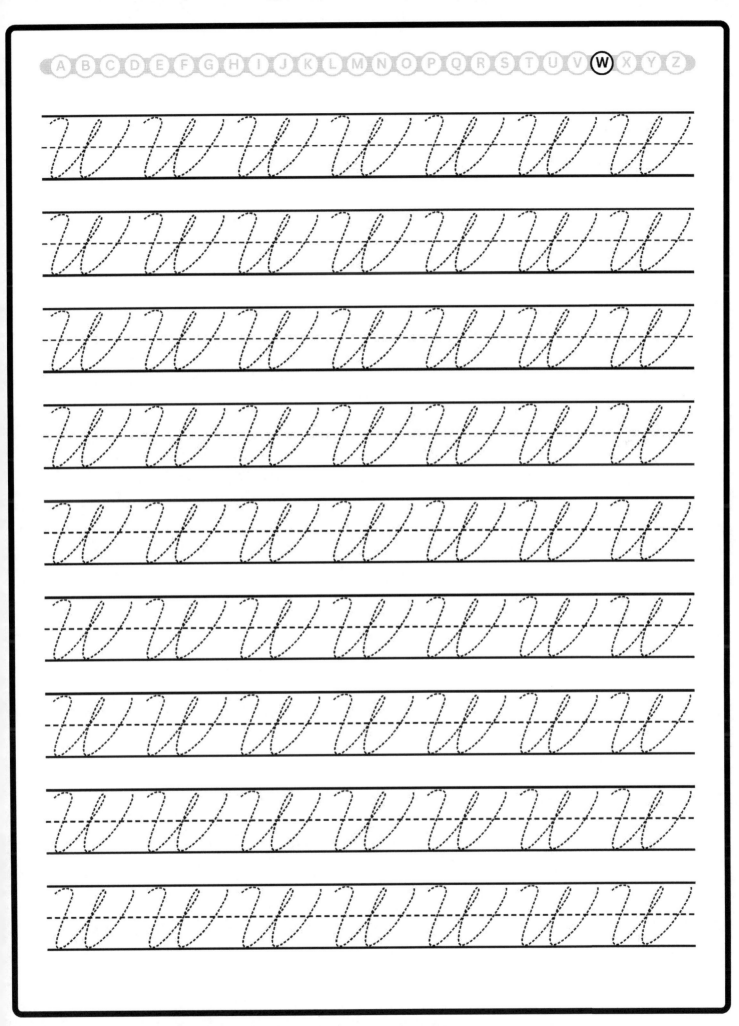

PRACTICE SHEET

WOLF

"I always do my best"

HOW TO WRITE LOWERCASE X

Trace inside the cursive letter by following the arrows

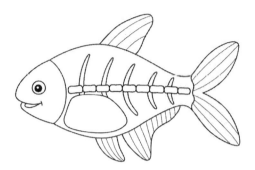

𝓍 𝓍 𝓍 𝓍 𝓍 𝓍 𝓍 𝓍 𝓍

HOW TO WRITE UPPERCASE X

Trace inside the cursive letter by following the arrows

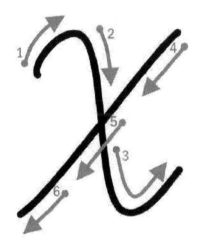

𝒳 𝒳 𝒳 𝒳 𝒳 𝒳 𝒳 𝒳

PRACTICE SHEET

X-RAY TETRA

"I am unique and special"

HOW TO WRITE LOWERCASE Y

Trace inside the cursive letter by following the arrows

𝒴 𝒴 𝒴 𝒴 𝒴 𝒴 𝒴 𝒴

HOW TO WRITE UPPERCASE Y

Trace inside the cursive letter by following the arrows

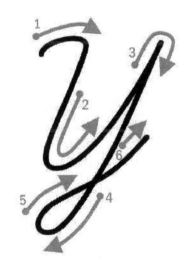

𝒴 𝒴 𝒴 𝒴 𝒴 𝒴 𝒴 𝒴

y y y y y y y

y y y y y y y

y y y

y

Y Y Y Y Y Y Y

Y Y Y

Y

PRACTICE SHEET

YELLOWJACKET

"I have the power to make a difference in the world"

HOW TO WRITE LOWERCASE Z

Trace inside the cursive letter by following the arrows

z z z z z z z z z z z z

HOW TO WRITE UPPERCASE Z

Trace inside the cursive letter by following the arrows

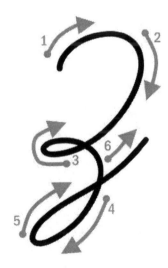

Z Z Z Z Z Z Z Z Z Z Z Z

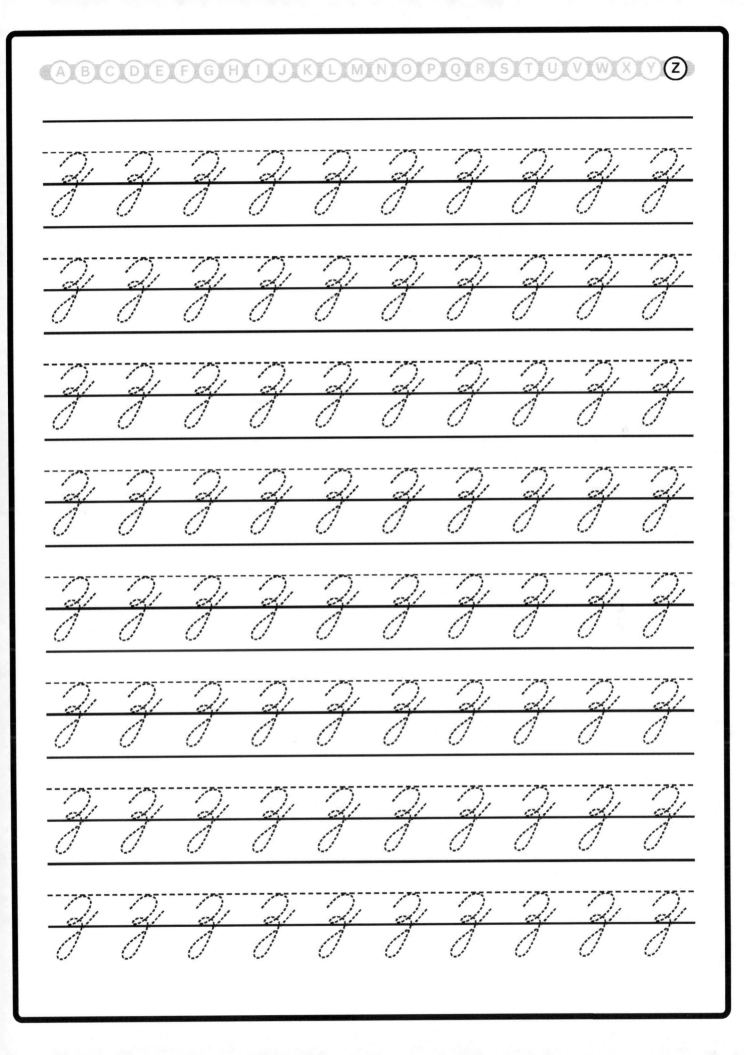

PRACTICE SHEET

ZEBRA

"I am proud of who I am"

SECTION 2

2

Writing in Words

Trace the words and then try practicing in the blank spaces below

Apple *Apple* *Apple*

Apple *Apple* *Apple*

apple *apple* *apple*

apple *apple* *apple*

Trace the words and then try practicing in the blank spaces below

Bear Bear Bear Bear

Bear Bear Bear

bear bear bear bear

bear bear bear

Trace the words and then try practicing in the blank spaces below

Cat Cat Cat Cat Cat

Cat Cat Cat

cat cat cat cat cat cat

cat cat cat cat

Trace the words and then try practicing in the blank spaces below

Dog Dog Dog Dog Dog

Dog Dog Dog

dog dog dog dog dog

dog dog dog

Trace the words and then try practicing in the blank spaces below

Egg Egg Egg Egg Egg

Egg Egg Egg

egg egg egg egg egg

egg egg egg

Trace the words and then try practicing in the blank spaces below

Fish Fish Fish Fish

Fish Fish Fish

fish fish fish fish fish

fish fish fish

Trace the words and then try practicing in the blank spaces below

Goat Goat Goat Goat

Goat Goat Goat

goat goat goat goat

goat goat goat

Trace the words and then try practicing in the blank spaces below

House House House

House House House

house house house

house house house

Trace the words and then try practicing in the blank spaces below

Igloo Igloo Igloo Igloo

Igloo Igloo Igloo

igloo igloo igloo igloo

igloo igloo igloo

Trace the words and then try practicing in the blank spaces below

Juice *Juice* *Juice* *Juice*

Juice *Juice* *Juice*

juice *juice* *juice* *juice*

juice *juice* *juice*

Trace the words and then try practicing in the blank spaces below

Kite Kite Kite Kite Kite

Kite Kite Kite

kite kite kite kite kite

kite kite kite

Trace the words and then try practicing in the blank spaces below

Lion Lion Lion Lion

Lion Lion Lion

lion lion lion lion

lion lion lion

Trace the words and then try practicing in the blank spaces below

Mouse Mouse Mouse

Mouse Mouse Mouse

mouse mouse mouse

mouse mouse mouse

Trace the words and then try practicing in the blank spaces below

Nest Nest Nest Nest

Nest Nest Nest

nest nest nest nest

nest nest nest

Trace the words and then try practicing in the blank spaces below

Owl Owl Owl Owl

Owl Owl Owl

owl owl owl owl owl

owl owl owl

Trace the words and then try practicing in the blank spaces below

Plane Plane Plane

Plane Plane Plane

plane plane plane

plane plane plane

Trace the words and then try practicing in the blank spaces below

Quail Quail Quail

Quail Quail Quail

quail quail quail quail

quail quail quail

Trace the words and then try practicing in the blank spaces below

Rose Rose Rose Rose

Rose Rose Rose

rose rose rose rose rose

rose rose rose

Trace the words and then try practicing in the blank spaces below

Sun Sun Sun Sun

Sun Sun Sun

sun sun sun sun sun

sun sun sun

Trace the words and then try practicing in the blank spaces below

Tent Tent Tent Tent

Tent Tent Tent

tent tent tent tent

tent tent tent

Trace the words and then try practicing in the blank spaces below

Up Up Up Up Up Up

Up Up Up

up up up up up up up

up up up

Trace the words and then try practicing in the blank spaces below

Van *Van* *Van* *Van*

Van *Van* *Van*

van *van* *van* *van*

van *van* *van*

Trace the words and then try practicing in the blank spaces below

Watch Watch Watch

Watch Watch

watch watch watch

watch watch watch

Trace the words and then try practicing in the blank spaces below

Xing Xing Xing Xing

Xing Xing

xing xing xing xing

xing xing xing

Trace the words and then try practicing in the blank spaces below

Yam Yam Yam Yam

Yam Yam Yam

yam yam yam yam

yam yam yam

Trace the words and then try practicing in the blank spaces below

Zebra Zebra Zebra

Zebra Zebra Zebra

zebra zebra zebra

zebra zebra zebra

SECTION

3

Writing in sentences

Trace the sentences and then try practicing in the blank spaces below

Apples taste good.

Apples taste good.

Apples are tasty.

Apples are tasty.

Trace the sentences and then try practicing in the blank spaces below

Boys like to play.

Boys like to play.

Boys love toys.

Boys love toys.

Trace the sentences and then try practicing in the blank spaces below

Cats meow.

Cats meow.

Cats purr.

Cats purr.

Trace the sentences and then try practicing in the blank spaces below

Dogs bark.

Dogs bark.

Dogs dig.

Dogs dig.

Trace the sentences and then try practicing in the blank spaces below

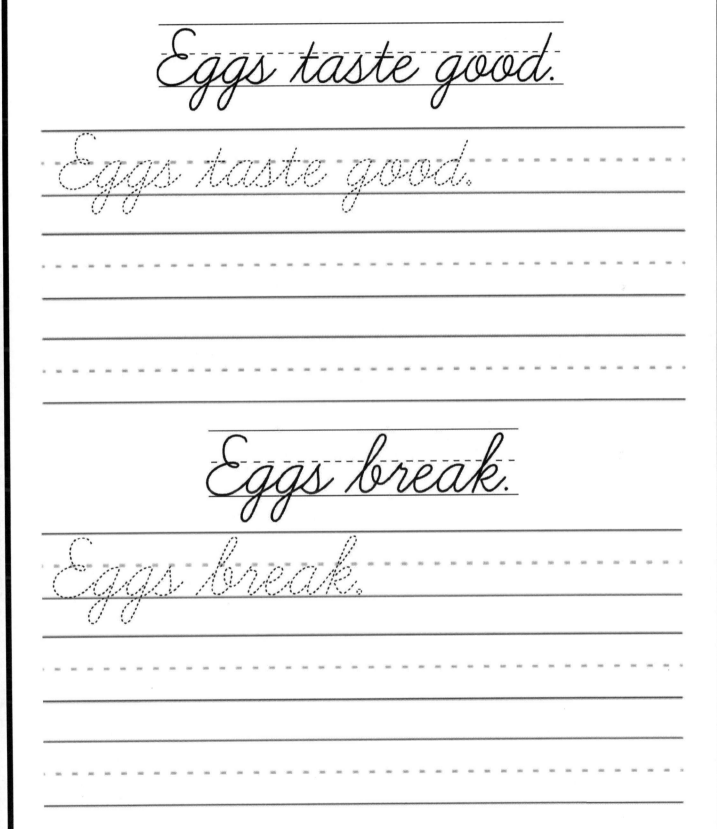

Eggs taste good.

Eggs taste good.

Eggs break.

Eggs break.

Trace the sentences and then try practicing in the blank spaces below

Football is fun.

Football is fun.

Fly a kite.

Fly a kite.

Trace the sentences and then try practicing in the blank spaces below

Go outside.

Go outside.

Giggle with me.

Giggle with me.

Trace the sentences and then try practicing in the blank spaces below

Hello friend.

Hello friend.

High in the sky.

High in the sky.

Trace the sentences and then try practicing in the blank spaces below

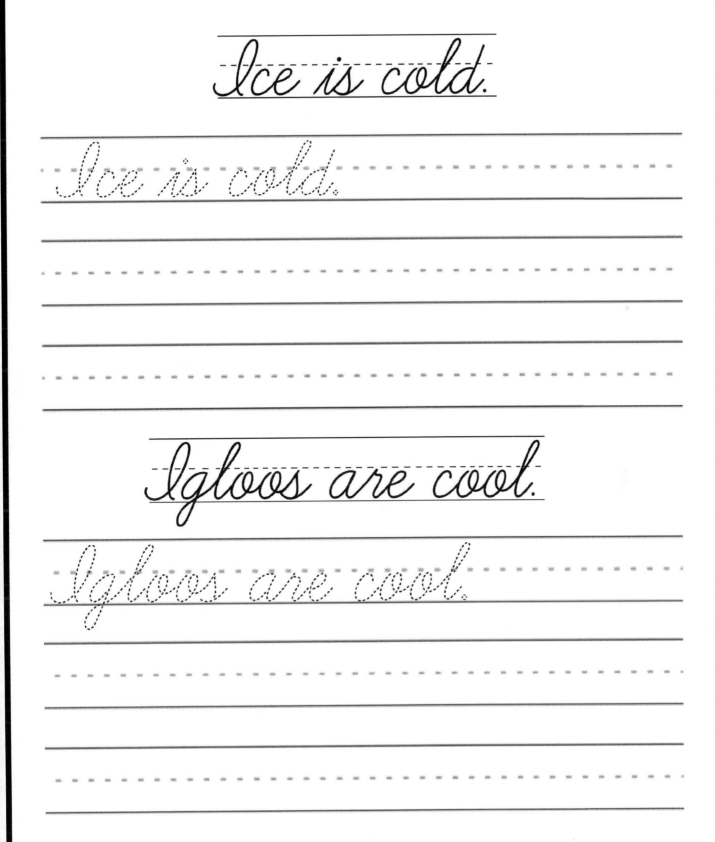

Ice is cold.

Ice is cold.

Igloos are cool.

Igloos are cool.

Trace the sentences and then try practicing in the blank spaces below

Jelly is good.

Jelly is good.

Jam is better.

Jam is better.

Trace the sentences and then try practicing in the blank spaces below

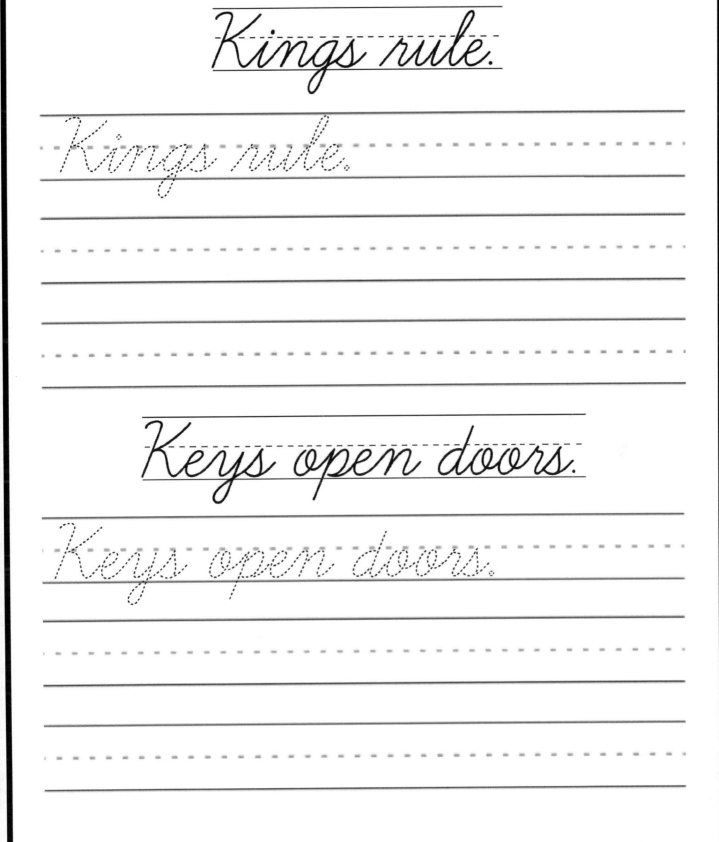

Kings rule.

Kings rule.

Keys open doors.

Keys open doors.

Trace the sentences and then try practicing in the blank spaces below

Leaves on trees.

Leaves on trees.

Lamps are bright.

Lamps are bright.

Trace the sentences and then try practicing in the blank spaces below

Mice love cheese.

Mice love cheese.

Monsters are scary.

Monsters are scary.

Trace the sentences and then try practicing in the blank spaces below

Noses itch.

Noses itch.

Nicely done.

Nicely done.

Trace the sentences and then try practicing in the blank spaces below

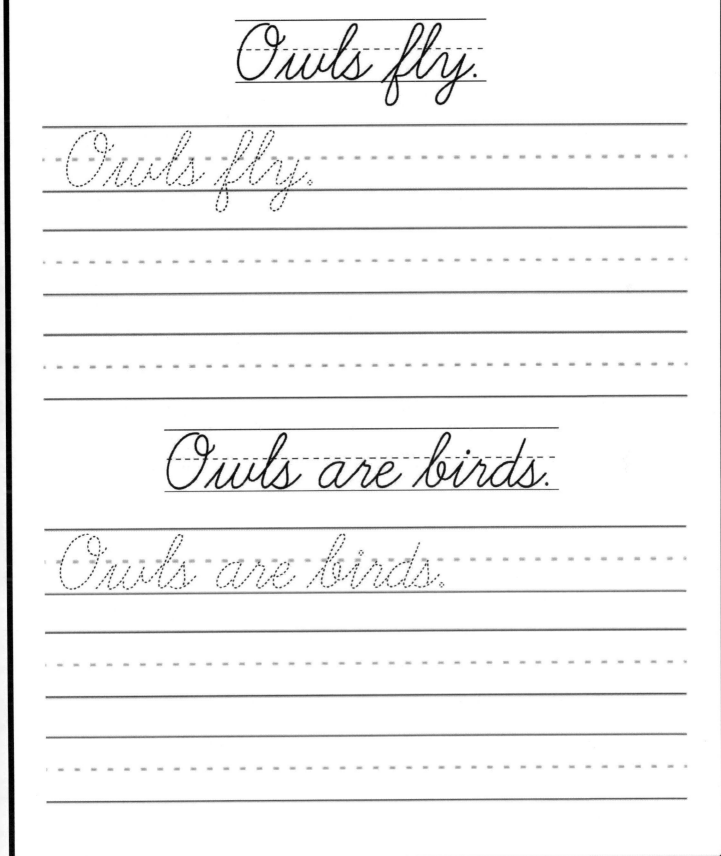

Owls fly.

Owls fly.

Owls are birds.

Owls are birds.

Trace the sentences and then try practicing in the blank spaces below

Pandas are cute.

Pandas are cute.

Puppies are playful.

Puppies are playful.

Trace the sentences and then try practicing in the blank spaces below

Questions are good.

Questions are good.

Quails are birds.

Quails are birds.

Trace the sentences and then try practicing in the blank spaces below

Roses smell good.

Roses smell good.

Red is pretty.

Red is pretty.

Trace the sentences and then try practicing in the blank spaces below

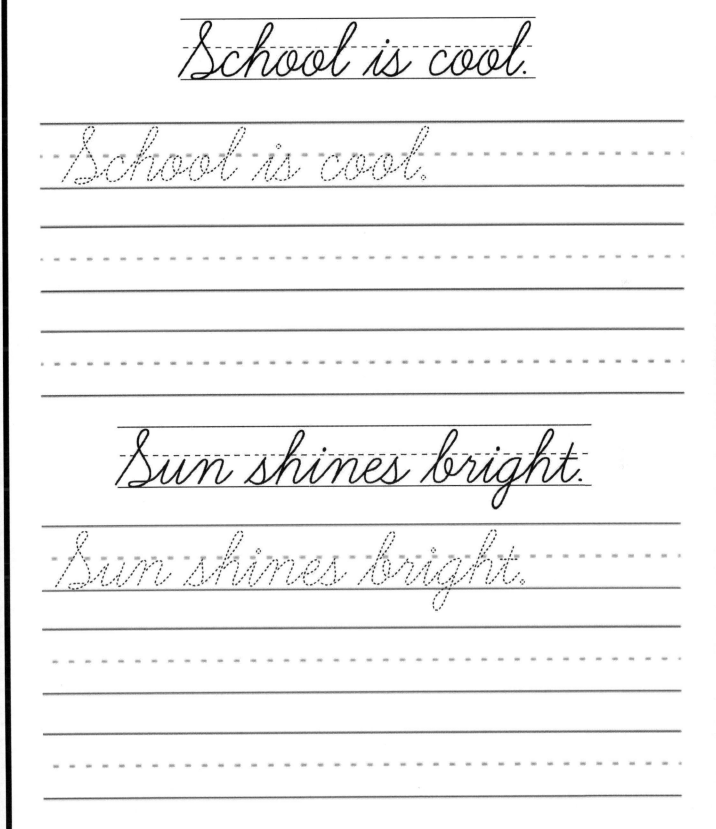

School is cool.

School is cool.

Sun shines bright.

Sun shines bright.

Trace the sentences and then try practicing in the blank spaces below

Toys are fun.

Toys are fun.

Tiny is cute.

Tiny is cute.

Trace the sentences and then try practicing in the blank spaces below

Up there.

Up there.

Up and down.

Up and down.

Trace the sentences and then try practicing in the blank spaces below

Vans are cool.

Vans are cool.

Violas sound nice.

Violas sound nice.

Trace the sentences and then try practicing in the blank spaces below

Watch me write.

Watch me write.

Write right.

Write right.

Trace the sentences and then try practicing in the blank spaces below

Xenon is a gas.

Xenon is a gas.

X-rays work.

X-rays work.

Trace the sentences and then try practicing in the blank spaces below

Yams are tasty.

Yams are tasty.

Yummy food.

Yummy food.

Trace the sentences and then try practicing in the blank spaces below

Zip zap zit.

Zip zap zit.

Zoom or boom.

Zoom or boom.

SECTION

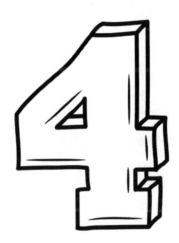

4

Bonus Round!
Jokes, longer sentences and more practice
pages

Trace the sentences and then try practicing in the blank spaces below

I can write words in

cursive now. It is fun!

I will write sentences in

cursive now. Let's do it.

Trace the sentences and then try practicing in the blank spaces below

I am full of keys, but

can't open any door.

What am I?

A piano

Trace the sentences and then try practicing in the blank spaces below

What music frightens

balloons? Pop music

Trace the sentences and then try practicing in the blank spaces below

What has 4 eyes but

can't see?

Mississippi

Trace the sentences and then try practicing in the blank spaces below

What fish only swims at night?

A starfish A starfish A starfish

What part of a fish weighs the most?

The scales The scales The scales The scales

Trace the sentences and then try practicing in the blank spaces below

What two things can you

never eat for breakfast?

Lunch and dinner

Trace the sentences and then try practicing in the blank spaces below

What do you call snakes with no clothes on?

Snaked Snaked Snaked Snaked

What's a frog's favorite drink?

Croak-a-cola Croak-a-cola Croak-a-cola

Trace the sentences and then try practicing in the blank spaces below

What starts with T, ends

with T and is filled with T?

Teapot

Trace the sentences and then try practicing in the blank spaces below

What do you call a girl with a frog on her head?

Lilly Lilly Lilly Lilly Lilly Lilly

What do you call a cow that eats your grass?

A lawn moo-er   A lawn moo-er

PRACTICE SHEET

PRACTICE SHEET

PRACTICE SHEET

AWARD CERTIFICATE

For your effort and practice in completing the book

Cursive Handwriting Workbook

_____

(Write your name on this line)

_____

Date

59512641R00128